# Anxiety The Book

A Practical Guide to Eliminating Anxiety and
Getting on with Your Life

**Carolyn G.A Ching**

Website: www.anxietythebook.com
Facebook page: @anxietythebook

Anxiety The Book:
A Practical Guide to Eliminating Anxiety and
Getting on with Your Life

Carolyn G.A Ching

Copyright © 2022 Carolyn G.A Ching

ISBN: 979-8-9858603-1-3

First Printing: March 2022

Purple Hibiscus Media
Carolyn G.A Ching
Kailua Kona
Hawaii 96740
www.anxietythebook.com

**Carolyn Ching is available to speak at your business or conference event on a variety of topics. She also holds retreats and personal breakthrough sessions on the Big Island of Hawaii and is available for personal and Zoom sessions. Call or Text (808) 4641519 for bookings and information.**

# Why Read This Book

Anxiety has become more prevalent over the past few years and diminishes the quality of life for many people dealing with it. There is no simpler way to make significant changes in your life and eliminate anxiety than by reading this book.

This book reveals the most effective methods to address the factors that are causing your anxiety, provides exercises and techniques that are easy to understand and use, and shows you how to create your own unique recipe for success. Like most things, anxiety arises from a combination of factors, and this book enables you to discover the things that have lead to your anxiety and gives you specific tips and techniques to deal with those factors.

Once you begin putting the information in this book into effect you will be able to step into a new chapter of your life!

**Are you ready to make lasting change and free yourself from anxiety?**

**If so, then let's begin taking the first steps today!**

This book has arisen from over twenty years of experience in helping people just like you to overcome anxiety. It is easy to follow and understand, enabling you to take the steps you need to make changes, at your own pace and with confidence. There are places for you to complete exercises and add your own notes' it's your book, your very own recipe for getting your life back!

# Written by a Leading Expert with over Twenty Years of Experience

**Carolyn G.A Ching** is a Certified Hypnotherapist and member of the ICBCH. Carolyn is also a Registered Nurse; Professional Counselor; Hypnotherapy, NLP (Neurolinguistic Programming), and Time Line Therapy Practitioner and Trainer. Carolyn is a popular speaker at conferences throughout the USA and Australia.

Carolyn G.A Ching is the expert other professionals come to study with and also the therapist other therapists come to for personal sessions. In addition to her twenty-plus years of private practice in Hawaii, she has also worked with celebrities at the Golden Door Health Retreat in Australia. Carolyn has specialized in helping people overcome anxiety since 2001. In this book, Carolyn explains everything you need to know in order to get over your anxiety in a way that is easy to understand. When you are finished with this book, you will have a new resource that you can tap into for the rest of your life.

Carolyn lives on the beautiful Big Island of Hawaii where she loves spending time by the ocean. She also enjoys spending time on the Sunshine Coast of Australia with her family.

**Do you want Carolyn G.A Ching to be the motivational speaker at your next event?**

**Call (808) 464 1519**

# What others are saying about this book

"This excellent book gives you all the tools and resources you need to overcome your anxiety and be free to enjoy your life again. If you buy just one book about anxiety, make sure its this one!"

____ Dr Richard Nongard, author of The Seven Most Effective Methods of Self- Hypnosis

"Carolyn Ching's engaging book is a must-read in these anxiety-inducing times. She provides practical advice and easy-to-follow exercises that will help you overcome your anxiety and live your best life."

____ Vera Stewart-Lutz, CHt, Solutions Hypnotherapy, Arizona

"FINALLY! An easy-to-read book with easy-to-understand techniques REAL people can use to get the results that they want! The simplicity of this book makes it easy for ANYONE to understand"

____ Kahikina (aka Polynesian Pirate), radio personality, KAPA Radio Hawaii

"Anxiety/fear of future possible events yet to unfold can keep one frozen in position or running in circles. Free yourself from needless suffering by following Carolyn's easy, effective, time-proven, and safe methods found within these helpful pages! Here's to your future finally being free of anxiety!"

____ Maggie M. Connor, olympian, master trainer

# Table of Contents

# CHAPTER ONE

## Anxiety Sucks! Exploring Anxiety

"I have anxiety," Megan said, as she slumped into my client chair. "And it sucks!"

I opened my notebook and asked her to tell me more about it.

"I'm finding it hard to deal with the kids, the house," she replied. "I'm snapping at my kids; I'm snapping at my husband. Every morning I wake up really early, and I've got this knot in my stomach; I just don't want to go to work. At night I don't sleep properly: I have thoughts running through my head all the time. I'm worried about everything, I'm exhausted, and I don't want to go anywhere. I'm so tired of being anxious all the time ..." And then she started to cry ...

1

If that sounds like you, you may be suffering from anxiety, and you definitely know one thing:

Anxiety sucks!

Some of the common symptoms of anxiety are:

- Palpitations
- Tingling sensations
- Dry mouth
- Difficulty sleeping
- Racing thoughts
- Sweaty palms
- Exhaustion
- Difficulty concentrating
- Irritability
- Muscle tension
- Knots or feelings of unease in the stomach

Anxiety is the feeling we get when we are worried or fearful about things that are about to happen or that we think could happen in the future. When we feel threatened, hormones such as adrenaline and cortisol are automatically secreted by the body. These hormones make us more alert so that we can act faster and also make the heart beat more rapidly, sending blood to where it's needed in the body quickly. This is known as the fight-or-flight response.

Like Megan, many of my clients experience anxiety, and the good news is that it can be overcome.

Jeremiah came into my office one day. He was a successful businessman in his mid-forties who liked to work out regularly.

"I keep getting heart palpitations," he said. "I keep getting this racing feeling in my body, and my thoughts just won't stop. I have this feeling like I'm getting breathless--like I can't breathe! I'm on the go all the time; everything is go, go, go, and then when I do stop, I can't relax because my head just won't stop. There's so much going on in my head all the time!"

I took a deep breath and asked him some questions:

- [ ] Are you a perfectionist?

- [ ] Do you have high expectations of yourself and-or others?

- [ ] Are you the strong one? The person other people come to for advice and help or to offload their problems on?

- [ ] Do you have difficulty saying no?

- [ ] Have one or both of your parents suffered from anxiety?

- [ ] Has there been an incident or incidents in the last two to three years where you have been out of control either due to an illness or injury, or due to something that's happened in your environment, to you, or people close to you?

- [ ] Have any loved ones passed away recently?

"Wow! How did you know?" he replied. "I'm definitely a perfectionist: I have high expectations of myself as well as the people that I work with. Just last year I lost a good friend as well as my father, but I've been so busy that I don't think I've had a chance to grieve properly!"

Saying yes to several of these questions is a classic recipe for developing anxiety. How many of these situations are true for you?

Write them here:

_____

_____

_____

_____

_____

The first thing I tell my clients--and what I'd also like to say to you--is this:

"It's okay! You're going to get through this. You're going to get your life back; in fact, it will be better than it was before, because of the changes you are about to make and the insights you've gained that you didn't have before. I have some tips and techniques that can help you to get through this, that can help you to get your life back on track, so that you are able to enjoy your life again."

Typically, my clients respond with a look of hope combined with disbelief because when you've been feeling as bad as they have for as long as they have, it seems like you'll never be able to get over it. The great news is that if you're willing to implement some new techniques and make some changes, you will get through this. Many of my clients, like Megan and Jeremiah, don't want to go on medication. They often tell me I am their last resort!

So who am I to be helping them, anyway?

I began my career as a Registered Nurse. In that capacity, I encountered people coming into the emergency room with symptoms of anxiety and panic attacks thinking they were having a heart attack. All we could do was say, "No, it's anxiety," and I was frustrated that we couldn't really help them, so I trained in Counseling, Hypnotherapy, Neuro-Linguistic Programming, and Time Line Therapy. As a therapist for the past twenty-plus years, I've had the privilege of working with a wide variety of people who have experienced the debilitating effects of anxiety on their lives. I have been able to successfully help them make the changes they need to make; I've experienced the joy of seeing them overcome anxiety and get on with their lives.

On a personal note, my mother suffered from anxiety for many years, and I myself have had times when I've experienced it. When my son was just eighteen months old, my first husband was diagnosed with cancer. For several years while he underwent chemotherapy and a bone marrow transplant, I had times when I found myself anxious about the future. Troubling thoughts echoed constantly in my head: "What if he dies and I'm left to bring our son up alone? What if my son develops the same thing? What if the bone marrow transplant doesn't work?" In short, I am no stranger to anxiety.

But anxiety doesn't arise only from severe medical crises. I've lived and worked in four countries, starting businesses in two of them. I know first-hand what it's like to be a perfectionist, to be the "strong one" others come to for advice. The techniques I am going to share with you are the same ones I needed in order to regain the balance and inner calm that enables me to face challenges and remain in a "good space." This book has arisen from a combination of all those factors, and it's my passion to bring it to you and help you get your life back.

These pages contain all the tips and techniques I teach my clients. They're easy to understand, and anyone can apply them. As you begin to implement the ideas, tips, and techniques in the following chapters, you are going to find that your anxiety reduces, and you start to feel better. If you consistently apply them, you will regain control of your life, have more energy, be able to experience the feeling of happiness and joy again, and get back to doing all the things you want and need to do. You will also have the knowledge and skills to prevent anxiety from taking over your life in the future.

By turning the page and reading the rest of this book, you'll gain insight and understanding into what's happening when you have anxiety. By doing the exercises and making simple changes, you will be able to eliminate anxiety and get on with your life!

# ∽ NOTES ∽

# CHAPTER TWO

## Benefits of Living a Life Free from Anxiety

According to the American Psychiatric Association it's estimated that approximately 30% of all adults in America will suffer from anxiety at some point in their life. In 2021 The World Health Organization started that 3.6% (approx 264 million people) worldwide have an Anxiety disorder.

Anxiety takes a physical and mental toll on people and often on the people around them, too. Left unaddressed, anxiety can become more pronounced and begin to feel like it's taking over your life: Sleeping becomes more difficult; worrying thoughts grow more frequent and more pronounced; the ability to concentrate diminishes; feelings of tension, restlessness, and jitteriness increase.

There may be dizziness, sweating, and appetite changes; hyper-vigilance often occurs.

Of course, every client wishes that I had a magic wand I could wave to make their anxiety disappear. It would be lovely if this were the case; however, in order to feel well again, there are some things that you will need to do differently!

Let's continue our story about Megan:

Once we had identified all of the factors pertaining to her anxiety and identified her symptoms, it was time for her to start putting some simple solutions in place. Although she was desperate to find a resolution for her anxiety without medication, Megan had difficulty taking time for herself every day to put into practice the elements needed to eliminate her anxiety. Like most people, she had great intentions; however, she would easily get distracted by the needs of her children, her boss at work, and the busy-ness of her life! Sometimes she would think to herself, "It's not so bad. It will go away. We all have our problems; this is just mine." Part of her believed that it would be selfish to put herself first and take time to do the exercises. She also worried, "What if it doesn't work? It might work for others and not me; maybe nothing will help." Another thought that stopped her from learning the techniques was "I'm too tired." These thought-patterns and beliefs were of course also part of the reason why she was experiencing anxiety in the first place.

After several weeks of intending to do the exercises and then feeling dismayed that yet another week had gone by without any change, she finally realized that she really did have to start making the changes herself to experience improvement.

I wonder if you've fallen into any of the issues that Megan had about making changes? Many of my clients have, but eventually, they realize that they really do want to be able to live a full and happy life again, and that only by implementing these new skills will they make it happen.

One of the first things that Megan did was to write a list of the benefits of not having anxiety. She printed this list out and kept one copy in her purse, one by her bed, and one at work. The list reminded her of why she was taking time to do this for herself and enabled her to feel hopeful about her future. With this motivation, Megan began to set a little bit of time aside for herself every morning as soon as she got up. She also set some alarms on her phone so that she could be reminded to do the quick yet transformative exercises during the day.

What are the benefits of living life without anxiety?

Prior to the first session with me, I ask my clients to write a list containing ten benefits of living life without anxiety. In the space below, write down ten benefits of living your life free from anxiety:

_____

_____

_____

_____

_____

_____

_____

_____

_____

_____

Now that you've completed your list, here are some common things that my clients write:

- Be myself
- Be free
- Have better relationships
- Feel safe
- Enjoy social gatherings and events
- Be more present
- Sleep better
- Enjoy my life
- Have more energy
- Feel more relaxed

- Feel happier in myself
- Better sex life
- Be able to travel again
- Be able to drive confidently

I'm sure you will find there are some similarities with your list.

Take a moment now to close your eyes and think of those benefits that you wrote. What will you see, hear, feel, and experience when you are free of anxiety? How will your life be different? Let yourself fully experience that.

Just reading her list once it was written motivated Megan to start using the techniques I'm going to share with you. The next chapter contains an overview of the information and practical exercises that will enable you to overcome your anxiety and start experiencing the benefits you have written on your list!

# ❧ NOTES ❧

# CHAPTER THREE

## The Seven Key Areas of Change and Creating your Individual Recipe for Success

F rom working with hundreds of clients over the last twenty-plus years, I've discovered that just as there is a combination of factors that lead to anxiety, there is also a combination of solutions. Many people are surprised at how quickly they begin to feel better once they start practicing the different tools and techniques that I'm sharing with you. Each chapter contains exercises for you to do and tools to implement. You will benefit most if you do the exercises with an open mind and are honest with yourself.

The key elements for reducing and ultimately eliminating anxiety are outlined below. Each will be fully explored in the coming chapters:

- Understanding the role of the unconscious mind and how to use it for health and wellbeing. Exploring the language we use in our mind, changing words of pressure to words of choice, and eliminating those pesky what-if thoughts. What we think, we become!

- Being kinder to yourself and learning to address perfectionism. Yes, you really can do it!

- Setting boundaries, recognizing when to say no, and learning how to say no. (It's easy! Really!)

- Breathing. Yes it's essential for a healthy life, and most of us don't realize we are perpetuating the fight-flight response by the way we breathe. Becoming aware of this and making small changes can have a profound effect on how we feel. In Chapter Seven, you'll learn the 5X5 Breathing Technique, which is fast, easy, and effective. We will also take a trip to Vegus (not Vegas!)

- Decreasing stress levels using the Sensory Relaxation Technique, which enables you to relax in any environment. It's quick and easy to use.

- Improving your ability to fall asleep and stay asleep, so that you can awaken refreshed, revitalized, and ready to start your day. In Chapter Nine, you will learn the Notebook Technique.

- Comprehending grief, its impact on anxiety, and how to get through it. Chapter Ten includes a practical exercise for letting go of grief.
- Other tips and magical techniques to eliminate the feeling of anxiety

**Your Individual Recipe for Success**

It's important to be aware that it's often a buildup of several things that cause anxiety, so eliminating anxiety calls for us to become aware of the combination of these elements and be willing to make several changes. We are going to create an individual recipe for success so that you know which combination of things is likely to work best for you. As you read through the following chapters, you will become aware of the issues that resonate with and relate to you, and you may wish to add things to your recipe for success.

Are you ready to change now? Then let's proceed!

If you didn't already answer these questions in Chapter One, answer them now as they will help determine which areas will be most effective for you to work on:

☐ Are you a perfectionist?

☐ Do you have high expectations of yourself and-or others?

☐ Are you the strong one? The person other people come to for advice and help or to offload their problems on?

☐ Do you have difficulty saying no?

☐ Have one or both of your parents suffered from anxiety?

☐ Has there been an incident or incidents in the last two to three years where you have been out of control either due to an illness or injury, or due to something that's happened in your environment, to you, or people close to you?

☐ Have any loved ones passed away recently?

I recommend that everyone works with the negative "what-ifs," the 5x5 Breathing Technique, and the Sensory Relaxation Technique before adding in the other items as appropriate for their personal situation. Of course, you may do all of the exercises in the book if you wish.

If you answered yes to "Are you a perfectionist?" or "Do you have high expectations of yourself and others?" then add the exercises in Chapter Five to your recipe for success.

If you answered yes to "Are you the strong one? The person other people come to for advice and help or to offload their problems on?" or "Do you have difficulty saying no?" then add the exercises in Chapter Six to your recipe for success.

If you answered yes to "Did one or both of your parents suffer from anxiety?" then add the exercises in the section entitled "Be Kind to Yourself" from Chapter Four to your recipe for success.

If you answered yes to "Has there been an incident or incidents in the last two to three years where you have been out of control either due to an illness or injury, or due to something that's happened in your environment, to you, or people close to you?" or if one of your loved ones has passed away recently, then add Chapter Ten to your recipe for success.

If sleep is an issue for you, then add Chapter Nine exercises to your recipe for success.

So let's create your recipe here:

1. What-if thoughts from Chapter Four (required)
2. 5x5 Breathing from Chapter Seven (required)
3. Sensory Relaxation from Chapter Eight (required)
4. _____
5. _____
6. _____
7. _____
8. _____
9. _____
10. _____

During the first week, begin using the exercises in steps 1, 2, and 3 above; then in the second week, add another exercise from your list so you are building on your skills. Continue adding new practices to your regimen until your recipe is in full effect.

# ∾ NOTES ∾

# CHAPTER FOUR

## The Unconscious Mind, What-if Thoughts, and Treating Yourself Kindly

Most people are familiar with the notion that we have a conscious mind and an unconscious (subconscious) mind. One of the first things to become aware of is your unconscious mind. Your unconscious mind is the part of you that is responsible for controlling your automatic bodily functions such as breathing, heartbeat, and blinking. It is also responsible for storing your memories. It houses your values, beliefs, and emotions, and it's the part of you that you don't have to think about.

The unconscious mind is creative, intuitive, irrational, and emotional. Because it's illogical, it can imagine anything you want, for example, wealth, health, and mood. It can also keep you stuck in negative behaviors as you continue to run negative belief patterns.

Your unconscious mind operates on its programming like a computer does, and it can be reprogrammed just like a computer. We are constantly reprogramming our unconscious mind through our experiences and self-talk. If we repeatedly tell ourselves that we are a failure or that we are a success, that we are happy or that we are anxious, that is what we become. What we tell ourselves, we become!

The conscious mind accounts for approximately ten percent of your mind. It is the part of you that is aware of what is going on right now. The conscious mind is logical and analytical, and it's where we spend most of our time. The conscious mind exercises willpower, and also analyses and evaluates whatever concern, situation, or issue has its attention. It is with our conscious mind that we make decisions and choices; however, those decisions are influenced by the information that is stored in our unconscious mind.

I like to use the metaphor of the unconscious mind being just like a five-year-old child in how it acts and reacts to things. I liken the conscious mind to being a big brother or sister. Thinking of the unconscious mind in this way helps us to easily make changes.

Whenever there is anxiety, there is always some negative thinking. Anxiety arises from a fear of something that hasn't even happened yet. You may already be aware of some negative thinking, but the negative thoughts that you are aware of are like the tip of an iceberg. There are many more thoughts that we are thinking that we are not consciously aware of yet.

These negative thoughts are usually "what-if" thoughts. They sound like this:

- "What if this goes wrong?"
- "What if that doesn't work?"
- "What if that happens?"

Your unconscious mind can't tell the difference between whether that is simply a thought or whether it's actually happening right now. For example, if you're thinking, "What if I have a terrible day at work today and my boss is mean to me?" your unconscious mind thinks that's actually happening to you right now, so it sends out stress chemicals (such as adrenaline) into the body.

Imagine saying to a five-year-old child, "What if you have a terrible day at school today and your teacher is mean to you?" That child simply would not want to go to school! Now imagine saying another five or ten negative "what-if" statements to that five-year-old, and you can imagine that the child would want to run away and hide rather than be around you.

Adrenaline and cortisol are the fight-and-flight chemicals. If there is an actual danger such as someone showing up at the front door with a shotgun or a bear crouching on your front porch, then your body is going to secrete adrenaline so that you can either fight whatever the danger is or run away from it.

When you are engaged in negative thinking, there is no bear on the porch, there is no one with a shotgun at your door, and so your body doesn't actually use those chemicals. You are left with your stress levels rising and the unused adrenaline simply circulating around the body.

When you have anxiety, the stress levels in your body have often been high for a long period of time, and you may find yourself in a hyper-alert stage where simple things trigger you: perhaps you hear a sudden noise such as a car backfiring or someone drops something, and you find yourself shaking and your heart pounding. Or perhaps someone says something, and you react by becoming angry or teary for no apparent reason. This can be as a result of multiple stressful incidents that have not been resolved, or of continuously putting stress and pressure on yourself by the language that you use in your mind.

So the first step to regaining your life is to make some changes in thinking. This won't happen overnight as it's probably been building up for years; however, it will happen and much sooner than you think!

The easiest way to start making changes in your thinking is to become aware of the "what-if" thoughts. When you notice one, tell yourself "Stop," then ask yourself, "Do I have proof?" If the answer is no--and it will almost always be no--let it go and turn it around to the positive opposite.

Example 1:

**What-If:** "What if I can't pay my rent this month?"

**STOP** (Say it out loud if you are on your own.)

**Do I have proof?** "Do I have proof right now this very minute that I can't pay my rent this month?"

**Answer:** "Well actually no because it's the 15th, and my rent is due on the 28th, and I still have some income due to come in."

**Turn it Around:** "What if the money comes in and I'm absolutely fine? What if I can pay the rent easily this month?"

You may not consciously believe the turn-around; however, your unconscious (five-year-old) mind needs to hear it.

Example 2:

**What-If:** "What if my partner is going to leave me?"

**STOP** (Say it out loud if you are on your own.)

**Do I have proof?** "Do I have proof right now this very minute that my partner is going to leave me?"

**Answer:** "No, right now things are going well."

**Turn it Around:** "What if we continue to enjoy a great relationship?"

You may not consciously believe the turn-around; however, your unconscious (five-year-old) mind needs to hear it.

Now complete the next 3 with your own thoughts:

**What-If:** What if _____

**STOP** (Say it out loud if you are on your own.)

**Do I have proof?** Do I have proof right now this very minute that.. _____

**Answer:** No, because_____

**Turn it Around:** What if_____

You may not consciously believe the turn-around; however, your unconscious (five-year-old) mind needs to hear it.

**What-If:** What if _____

**STOP** (Say it out loud if you are on your own.)

**Do I have proof?** Do I have proof right now this very minute that.. _____

**Answer:** No, because_____

**Turn it Around:** What if_____

You may not consciously believe the turn-around; however, your unconscious (five-year-old) mind needs to hear it.

**What-If:** What if _____

**STOP** (Say it out loud if you are on your own.)

**Do I have proof?** Do I have proof right now this very minute that.. _____

**Answer:** No, because_____

**Turn it Around:** What if_____

You may not consciously believe the turn-around; however, your unconscious (five-year-old) mind needs to hear it.

If you begin to do this with all the "what-ifs" that you notice, you will feel considerably better within one-to-three weeks. Some people find that in the first few days of carrying out this exercise, they feel as though they are getting worse. If this occurs, it Is simply because you are noticing just how many negative "what-if" thoughts you are actually doing. Before this exercise you were not even conscious of many of these thoughts that were having a negative effect on your body and distressing your unconscious mind.

**Treat Yourself Kindly**

When you have anxiety, you may be increasing the stress levels in our body by putting stress and pressure on yourself with the language that you use in your mind. Words like **have to, must, should, ought to**, and got to all put pressure on you, and you can end up feeling like a deer trapped in headlights. Using words instead like **I can, I might, I wonder what it would be like, I wonder if I can, let's see,** and **it will be nice to** opens us up to choices.

Notice the difference in these statements:

**Pressure:** "I have to run five miles on the treadmill today."

**Choice:** "Let's see if I can run five miles on the treadmill today."

**Pressure:** "I should finish the reports by lunchtime."

**Choice:** "It will be nice to finish the reports by lunchtime."

Think of three times you have used these words of pressure and then reframe them to words of choice:

**Pressure:** I (should, must, ought to, got to, have to)

_____

**Choice:** (I can, I might, I wonder what it would be like to, I wonder if I can, let's see, it will be nice to)

_____

**Pressure:** I (should, must, ought to, got to, have to)

**Choice:** (I can, I might, I wonder what it would be like to, I wonder if I can, let's see, it will be nice to)

**Pressure:** I (should, must, ought to, got to, have to)

**Choice:** (I can, I might, I wonder what it would be like to, I wonder if I can, let's see, it will be nice to)

If you use these words of pressure regularly, begin to make a concerted effort to remove them from your vocabulary and use words of choice instead.

Jeremiah, the client mentioned in Chapter One, thought he was doing the right thing for his health and well-being by going to the gym daily and working out. What we discovered is that Jeremiah was using words of pressure whilst at the gym: "I should be lifting heavier weights. I have to do at least ten miles on the treadmill today. I have to do twenty repetitions today!" Then he would berate himself if he did not live up to his goals and expectations.

Now imagine for a moment telling a five-year-old, "You should be lifting heavier weights. You have to do at least ten miles on the treadmill today. You have to do twenty repetitions today!" That five-year-old would not want to go to the gym, let alone do anything while there! And

30

they certainly wouldn't be having fun! Now imagine saying to the five-year-old, "It would be fun to lift heavier weights today. Let's see if we can do ten miles on the treadmill today. I wonder if we can do twenty repetitions today" It's a very different feeling when you use words of choice.

In addition to using words of pressure, many of us are not kind to ourselves in our thought patterns. Often we run dialogue such as "I'm not good enough. I'm not intelligent enough. I'm not XX enough." Imagine telling a five-year-old child, "You have to go to school today. What if you have a terrible day? What if nobody wants to play with you? You're not as smart or as good-looking as the other kids. Everyone else does things better than you!" That child is certainly not going to want to go to school today, and if they do go to school after you've told them all of that, they are likely to have a rough day!

We think nothing of telling ourselves things like this repeatedly, day in, day out, in our own minds, and then we wonder why we feel anxious or lack confidence in certain situations.

Let's practice turning around "I'm not enough" statements.

1. I'm not good enough.

Now turn it around: I am good enough.

2. I'm not smart enough.

Now turn it around: I am smart enough.

Write your own examples here:

1. I'm not _____

Now turn it around:

I am _____

2. I'm not _____

Now turn it around:

I am _____

3. I'm not _____

Now turn it around:

I am _____

The turn-around phrase is great to use as an affirmation. Write it on a post-it note and stick it on your mirror. Write it in lipstick on your mirror--guys can do this too!--and read it every morning and every evening. Put a post-it sticker on your desk or in your wallet, on the back of your work ID badge, anywhere where you will be reminded of it regularly.

When you first read this chapter, you will start to become aware of the things you are thinking/ saying to yourself that are creating anxiety. My advice is to focus on the "what-if" thinking for a week; notice the "what-if" thoughts and turn them around even if you don't consciously believe the turnaround.

Once you have done that for a week start to look at the "should, must, ought to, have to, got to," and change that language! Add this in week two.

In week three, begin to look at the "I am not XX enough" thinking. Turn it around and begin using the positive as an affirmation to motivate you. Continue to improve your thought processes, while still working with the "what-ifs" and ensuring you are using language of choice, not of pressure.

If you enjoy using affirmations, saying them to yourself throughout the day can be helpful. Ensure that your affirmations are positive and focus on what is wanted.

Here are some great affirmations:

"I am safe and well."

"Today is a great day."

"I am calm and relaxed."

"Everyday in every way I'm getting better and better"

By the end of week one, you will already be noticing some positive changes; as you continue to build on your skills, the improvement will continue.

## ∾ NOTES ∾

# CHAPTER FIVE

## Perfectionism

As I mentioned in the last chapter, the analogy I like to use is that our unconscious mind acts and reacts in a similar way to a real five-year-old child. I ask my clients if they know a real live five-year-old child, perhaps a relative or a neighbor. If not, I suggest they may wish to give their unconscious mind a name and imagine it as a real five-year-old child.

The easiest way to start treating yourself kindly and working with your unconscious mind in the way that it needs to be worked with is to check in regularly with yourself by asking, "Could I say this to a real live five-year-old child and have the child be happy and healthy?" If the answer is no, do not say it to yourself.

Many of my clients have reported that thinking of their unconscious mind as a five-year-old child and giving it an actual name has really made it very easy for them to change the way they talk to themselves in their mind.

Many of us started to talk negatively to ourselves because of voices from the past; whether it's a parent, an older sibling, a teacher, or any childhood authority figure who may have been negative or treated us harshly, it's natural to internalize that criticism and continue it into adulthood. However, that person is long gone, and that situation is long gone--and yet we are still continuing that negative legacy. Now is the time to STOP and become a loving parent to yourself.

**Perfectionism**

Many people who suffer from anxiety are perfectionists and either have high expectations of themselves or high expectations of others--and sometimes both. This can lead to dissatisfaction with ourselves and others, and ultimately to burnout in careers, difficulties in family or married life, and also self-image issues.

When you are a perfectionist, you often take on more than you need to, purely because nobody else does "it" to the same standard that you do. It seems easier to take on larger workloads than to delegate and then worry that someone else will not do a good job, or have to spend time checking or redoing part of their work because you are not satisfied with it.

Perfectionism is often where the language of pressure comes in. Perfectionists tend to say or think things like,

"I've got to get this done today" or "I have to make sure this is perfect."

If you are a perfectionist, then be aware that your 100% is everybody else's 120%! One of the things you need to do to bring down the stress levels is to bring that percentage down from 100% to 80%. When you perform at 80% you will still be performing at everybody else's 100%! However, you will begin to feel much less rushed, stressed, and dissatisfied.

Many perfectionists feel resentful that others won't do things to their standards. They often think, "Poor me--I have to do everything."

The perfectionist is often:

- stressed at having to do too much
- stressed by trying to fit too much in with not enough time
- frustrated at having to redo things that others have already done
- using the language of pressure rather than the language of choice

Start by dropping your expectations of yourself by 10%. This can be difficult--I know, I've been there! Start by asking yourself, "Will any harm come to anyone or anything if I do not do this to my 100%? Is anyone in danger if I do this at 90%?" If the answer is no (and for most things the answer will be no), take a deep breath and walk away: hand the paperwork in without rechecking it, allow your spouse to chop the veggies or vacuum the floor however they want to do it, allow your kids to be responsible for their own homework or packing up their own toys. Even if you are not happy because it's not how you would do it, take a deep breath and focus on something else!

When we are continually redoing what someone else has done we are actually saying to them,

"You're not good enough." I'm sure this is not the message that you wish to give to your partner, children, and co-workers.

I had a client many years ago--let's call her Mary--she had anxiety. Her marriage was in trouble; she was complaining that her husband never vacuumed the house properly, that he would always miss the corners. Because of this she could never ask him to do it, and if he did it, she would always follow behind and redo it. She had to do everything herself; he never willingly helped out.

I told her that it's important to realize that everyone is doing their 100%. We all interpret the world differently; therefore, somebody will miss something that we see, and we may miss something that they see. It is important to treat everyone with respect. If someone does something differently, take a deep breath and accept that difference! Yes, this takes practice, but you will become happier and less stressed.

When Mary realized that she had been treating her husband as if he was not good enough and not capable, she changed her way of doing things--and you can, too.

Once you have managed to drop your perfectionism and expectations of others by 10% (focus on this for 1-2 weeks), then drop them another 10%. REMEMBER your 80% is everyone else's 100%!

# ❧ NOTES ☙

# CHAPTER SIX

## Boundaries

Many people experiencing anxiety have not set clear boundaries for themselves. This can occur in any area of life: family, relationships, work.

Often the person with anxiety is a "strong" person whom other people come to for help or for advice with their own problems. This person is often kindhearted and generous, and will say yes to helping others, even to their own detriment.

John was one of my clients in Australia. He was great at working with cars and enjoyed tinkering with his old MG at home for fun. Over the years people started to ask him to check their cars; a friend would say, "It's making a noise--could you just check that for me?" or "I don't have enough money to get my car fixed--could you take a look at it for me?" John was brought up to always be helpful to others, so he would automatically say yes even if it meant he lost out on time with his wife and kids at the weekend or it meant that he didn't have time to work on his own car.

Eventually he became so fed up that he didn't want to work on cars at all and became anxious when friends called, fearing it was another job he didn't have time to do. He found himself not wanting to socialize as he felt obligated to say yes if acquaintances asked for help.

I explained to John that there are three questions to ask yourself with everything you do:

- Do I want to do this?
- Do I personally need to do this?
- For what purpose would I do this?

If the answers are:

- No, I do not want to do this.
- I do not personally need to do this.
- The only purpose is that someone else wants/needs it.
- ... then say NO!

Many people find it difficult to say NO, yet it's only a two-letter word! Once you learn how to say NO, you will wonder why you haven't been doing this for years!

To say NO, get the NO out first:

"No. Thank you for asking, but I really can't help."

"No. Thank you for asking, but I simply can't come."

Practice saying these statements, and if the other person continues to ask why, repeat the statements like a broken record.

If you begin to give reasons or make excuses the other person has information to manipulate you with. For example, the conversation might go like this:

Question: Can you look at my car today?

Response: No, sorry, I have to take the kids to sports practice.

Question: That's okay; I'll swing by once you're home tonight.

John thought he was saying NO by telling his friends, "I don't really have time this week because the kids have basketball practice." However, his friends would still bring their cars and say, "Just fit it in when you can."

I explained to John that the word "NO" needs to be clear; this is why we say it first.

The "thank you for asking" helps the NO response to be easily accepted. If the person continues to ask simply repeat, "No. Thank you for asking; I cant help." With no other details or explanation, the NO will eventually be accepted.

John worried that his friends wouldn't like him or respect him if he said no to helping them. In fact, the opposite usually occurs. True friends respect you for being honest. The people who are not true friends or those who like to manipulate others will continue to ask until they realize that you now have a boundary in place--and then they will simply move on to someone else. Occasionally it feels as though you are losing friends, but in fact the people you are losing are not friends. They are simply people who have been using you.

I also explained to John that every time you say yes to something that your unconscious five-year-old already knows is something you don't want to do, something you don't personally need to do, and for which the only purpose is to please someone else, then your unconscious mind feels like you're letting it down, like you don't count, and then stress begins to build. If you go ahead and do that activity anyway, you will find that you don't enjoy it, you feel resentful, and your stress levels increase.

John was not sure that he could use this new way of responding; however, he knew he had to do something because his wife and children were suffering, and he was too. So the very next week when a friend asked for help with the car, John ran the questions through his mind:

"Do I want to? No!"

"Do I personally need to? No!"

"For what purpose would I do this? Because my friend expects it!--It helps only my friend, not me!"

So he said, "No. Thank you for asking, but I really can't help."

His friend looked at him and said, "Okay, I'll take it to the garage," and continued with the conversation.

John was amazed at just how easy it was to say NO. Several months later he reported back to me that his life was back on track: he had time to go out and have fun with the kids and his wife, and they were even planning a vacation. Yes, he had lost two "friends," but he realized they weren't true friends anyway, as they were only there when they needed something from him. John shared that he had also started using this technique at work and saying NO to extra work loads.

Now sometimes when we ask those three questions:

- Do I want to?
- Do I personally need to?
- For what purpose would I do this?

the answers could be:

"No, I don't want to."

"Yes, I do personally need to."

and "The purpose is ultimately for me."

In this case, even though the "want to" is a no, there is a positive benefit for you in the answers; therefore, the right thing would be to go ahead and do it

Here are some examples of that thought process:

"Do I want to go for a walk today?"

"No, I don't want to."

"Do I personally need to go for a walk today?"

"Yes, I probably do."

"For what purpose would I go for a walk today?"

"Well, because I haven't been this week, and I want to stay healthy."

"Do I want to go to work today?"

"No."

"Do I personally need to go to work today?"

"Yes."

"For what purpose would I go to work today?"

"Because I really do need the income in order to pay my bills."

When we consciously realise that there is actually a positive to doing the activity even though we might not want to, we find ourselves doing that activity with a different frame of mind and much less stress.

What things do you have difficulty saying NO to?

Run a few examples for yourself and practice giving the NO response next time you are asked.

⊙ Write your name here _____

_____

can you _____?

Ask yourself:

Do I want to? _____

(Write your answer here)

Do I personally need to? _____

(Write your answer here)

For what purpose would I do this? _____

_____

(Write your answer here)

Then practice saying, "No. Thank you for asking, but I

really can't _____ "

_____

⊙ Write your name here _____

_____

can you _____?

Ask yourself:

Do I want to? _____

(Write your answer here)

Do I personally need to? _____

(Write your answer here)

For what purpose would I do this? _____

(Write your answer here)

Then practice saying, "No. Thank you for asking, but I

really can't _____ "

⊙ Write your name here _____

_____

can you _____?

Ask yourself:

Do I want to? _____

(Write your answer here)

Do I personally need to? _____

(Write your answer here)

For what purpose would I do this? _____

(Write your answer here)

Then practice saying, "No. Thank you for asking, but I

really can't _____ "

It can feel scary or uncomfortable the first few times you say NO, but persevere because very soon, you will have more time and energy to do the things that you want to do, and you will also begin to realize that the people around you respect you for being able to say NO.

Gemma was in her late twenties. She worked for a large company and really wanted to get a promotion. In order to achieve this, she said yes to everything that was asked of her. She spent evenings and weekends at work, and was beginning to feel overwhelmed, resentful, and anxious. She rarely had time to go out with her friends and said she felt "like a hamster on a wheel," always running but never getting anywhere. She felt anxious about going to work and not being able to cope with the workload.

I explained to Gemma that if you always say yes, people do not have to respect you; they do not even have to think about you! Each time a task needed to be done her boss simply knew Gemma would do it, so she could just hand it over no matter what it was, secure in the knowledge that "Gemma will do this. Gemma will fix this. Gemma is here in the evening, so she can take care of that. Gemma will work the weekend--no problem!" No consideration was given as to whether Gemma could handle the workload or work extra hours. So in fact Gemma's boss didn't even have to think or wonder if she could do a task; the boss just handed it off to her fully expecting it to be done.

Once you learn to say NO, the other person has to think about you; they have to consider if you will be able to assist. Once Gemma learned to say NO, her boss had to think: "I wonder if Gemma can do this; I hope Gemma can help us on this project." If you say no (in this case to the boss), that person has to either do the task themselves, or delegate it to someone else; they become responsible for the issue/task themselves. From this point onwards, acknowledgement and recognition grows in regard to the things that you actually say yes to.

When we first talked about boundaries, Gemma was very reluctant to change her ways. She really did believe that saying yes to everything her boss asked her to do would put her in line for the promotion. Gemma worked on her negative "what if's," used the Notebook Technique at night, and found that at least her sleep was improving. She was beginning to feel better, but she still spent all her time at work.

As an aside, we discovered that Gemma regularly drank two coffees in the morning and at least two energy drinks every afternoon to keep herself going. Once we discussed the impact of these on her anxiety, she stopped the energy drinks and cut her coffee down to one a day.

The crunch came when someone else who had been at the company for only six months was given the promotion and Gemma was asked if she could help her settle into the new role! Gemma ended up taking two weeks off work for stress leave. During the first week, she slept and cried. After this, she spent some time with her friends to relax and some time alone to work on ways to put her boundaries in place and resolve her anxiety. She decided to start looking for other jobs.

Once Gemma went back to work, she started to use the Three Questions Technique, and she began to say NO to some of the tasks that were asked of her. The first few times she did this, she found herself waiting for backlash. The first time she said NO to her boss, the boss didn't hear her. Gemma repeated herself and made it clear that she did not have time to take on that task. Gemma began to ask herself, "Do I want to stay late at work in the evening? Do I personally need to stay late at work in the evening? For what purpose would I stay late in the evening?" As a result, she decided to go home at six pm every evening regardless of whether she had finished her tasks for the day or not. Gemma asked herself the same questions about working weekends and of course discovered that she would much rather be spending time at home or with her friends so she stopped working weekends. Gemma was surprised and delighted at how much better she felt. Her anxiety was diminishing, her social life was improving, and--although she had been looking at other jobs--she was offered a promotion at her own company within four months of having changed her way of doing things. Gemma reported back to me, "If I had known that this would work so well, I would have implemented it the first time we talked about it!"

# ⚲ NOTES ⚲

# CHAPTER SEVEN

## Breathing

Breathing is crucial to life, yet many of us do not breathe properly. Often our breath is shallow and from the chest upwards, rather than deep, coming from the belly.

I live in Hawaii, which is awesome for my clients there, because the local Hawaiian people breathe properly! They breathe deeply and from the belly. When Captain Cook first arrived on the Big Island of Hawaii, the locals thought he was a ghost because his skin was white and he breathed very shallowly, very superficially--and so they called him ha'ole which means without breath! This is why the Hawaiians still refer to White people as haoles.

One of the favorite places for Hawaiians to visit is Vegas as there is no legal gambling in Hawaii, but rather than talk about Vegas, we are going to talk about Vagus! To be specific: the Vagus nerve! It is the longest cranial nerve in the body and runs from the brainstem through the neck and chest down into the abdomen. The Vagus nerve is an important part of the parasympathetic nervous system, which works at switching off the fight/flight response. The parasympathetic nervous system is often known as the "rest and digest" system, and helps to make us feel calmer and more relaxed.

When we have anxiety, we breathe rapidly and shallowly from the chest upwards, and this promotes the fight/flight mode in the body by activating the sympathetic nervous system. If you are in a situation in which you feel anxious, breathing slowly and deeply can give you some instant relief as it helps to ease the body back into the parasympathetic mode.

**5x5 Breathing Technique**

One of the first things to do when you realise that you are breathing rapidly and shallowly or when you feel the very first symptoms of anxiety in your body is to let out a big sigh, "haaaaaaaaaaaaa"!

Next, begin to breathe slowly and deeply from your belly.

Count to five while you are inhaling. (Yes, this means you have to slow your breathing down.)

Hold your breath to the count of five. (If five is too difficult initially, count to three or four.)

Exhale slowly and fully to the count of five.

Do this for a total of five breaths.

I call this 5x5 Breathing as it is very simple to remember that way.

Practice 5x5 Breathing every day. Do one round as soon as you wake up, and then set an alarm on your phone for five random times during the day. When the alarm sounds, practice one round of 5x5 Breathing. This will help you to become aware of how you are breathing throughout the day.

The 5x5 Breathing is also useful in times when you feel stressed or anxious and will quickly help you to feel calmer.

Check in with yourself regularly throughout the day to see if you are breathing from your belly or are engaging in shallow breathing from the chest upwards. When you breathe deeply and from the belly, remember that your body switches into the parasympathetic or healing rest/digest mode, moving out of fight/flight, and so our goal is to make this the preferred way of breathing.

**Humming and Chanting**

The Vagus nerve is also connected to our laryngeal muscles (voice box). If we stimulate the Vagus nerve by humming or chanting, the vibration enables the Vagus nerve to send signals to the mind and body to relax and move to the parasympathetic nervous system. It really doesn't matter what you chant. Eastern religions are known for their chants, but if you are more comfortable with English, you can simply chant a mantra such as "by changing my thoughts, I'm changing my world."

Here are a few examples of mantras to chant:

- "OM" Studies have found that chanting OM for ten minutes can relax the mind and body, providing calm and peace.
- "Om mane Padme hum"
- "Nam myoho renge kyo" There is an interesting clip on YouTube with Tina Turner demonstrating this.
- "Om Shanti Shanti Shanti"

Humming a favorite tune to yourself has a similar effect to chanting. You can hum anything! As a side note, if ever you are having difficulty with a bowel movement, hum a tune, any tune! It will help.

## ∽ NOTES ∽

# CHAPTER EIGHT

## Relaxation

I n order to bring our stress levels back down to the normal range so that we are able to cope much more easily with life, we need to practice relaxation. Many people think they have to allocate a long period of time for relaxation, or that it's too difficult, or that they have to be somewhere that is quiet. None of this is true! The relaxation exercise that I am going to share with you here is brief yet very effective. It will take approximately five minutes to do; however, if you are able to rest for a few more minutes, do so.

### Sensory Relaxation

This exercise helps to stop the head chatter that is often present with anxiety and bring the stress levels down. It incorporates the sounds around us so that we can successfully learn to relax even in a noisy environment.

59

It's a good idea to record this relaxation exercise to your voice memo on the phone so that you can simply play it and listen to it. I will also be making a free audio of it available on www.anxietythebook.com After just a few short weeks of doing this daily, you will remember the exercise and won't need the voice recording anymore. After fourteen to twenty-one days of practicing this exercise, you will find that as soon as you roll your eyes up and begin to expand into your peripheral vision, you will already begin to feel yourself relaxing.

Find a place to sit comfortably.

Pick a spot out in front of you which is up above eye level (e.g. where the wall meets the ceiling or a spot on the ceiling). Roll your eyes up and focus on that spot, allowing your vision to expand around to the sides (peripheral vision).

Whilst still looking at the spot:

Concentrate on noticing four different things you can see in your peripheral vision, such as colors, shapes, or objects.

Then listen closely for four sounds that you can hear around you.

Still staring at that spot focus on four things you can feel, such as your breathing, chair, clothing, hands, or feet.

Close your eyes.

Remember three things you saw around you.

Listen carefully for three sounds around you.

Focus on three things that you can feel.

Open your eyes and focus on the same spot, expanding your peripheral vision again.

Notice two things you can see in your peripheral vision.

Listen for two sounds around you.

And still staring at that spot, focus on two things you can feel.

Close your eyes.

Remember one thing you saw.

Listen carefully for one new sound or the sound of your breathing.

Focus on the sensation of your breathing.

Continue to relax for a few minutes if you have time.

**Relaxation: A Case Study**

Brad was one of my clients who was anxious about flying. He had to fly frequently for work, and he had gotten to the point where he was contemplating changing jobs because he no longer wanted to travel. He loved his job yet had started feeling anxious every time he was on a plane, and that was no fun.

At the first session, the questions from Chapter Three highlighted that Brad had become a father nine months previously; since then he had been anxious about flying, worrying that if anything happened to him, his wife and child would be left alone. He had never had a bad experience flying, but a friend in high school years ago had lost his father in a light aircraft crash.

In conjunction with changing the negative "what-if" thoughts that Brad was engaging in, we also talked about using the Sensory Relaxation Process and the 5x5 Breathing when he is on a plane. Additionally, we created a Resource Anchor as described in Chapter Eleven.

The combination of turning the negative "what-if" thoughts around and using the Sensory Relaxation and 5x5 Breathing, both at home and when traveling, cleared the anxiety. He found himself able to travel comfortably again. Brad also used his Resource Anchor the first two times he went on a plane but didn't need to use it again after that.

Remember to set your phone alarm and practice the 5x5 Breathing five times a day. Be sure to practice the Sensory Relaxation Process once a day in order to start returning your stress levels to the normal range and bringing your body back into the parasympathetic mode.

It's also useful to use Sensory Relaxation if you've had a stressful phone call or experience in order to reduce the anxious feelings.

If you have trouble falling asleep or staying asleep at night, use the Notebook Technique, which incorporates the Sensory Relaxation as described in Chapter Nine.

## Being Present

When you have anxiety, a common symptom is racing thoughts in your mind--that head-chatter that just won't switch off. One of the ways to be able to switch this off and relax is to learn to be present in the moment. How often do you have a conversation with someone and you are already trying to work out your response without even listening to what they are saying? How often do you take a moment to literally stop and smell the flowers around you, or to appreciate the sight of a bird in the yard, or to simply enjoy the invigorating feeling of cold winter air on your face? Often we are so busy just being busy that we don't appreciate the world around us or the people in it.

One of the wonderful things about living in Hawaii is that the local people are very connected to the land, to the ocean, to everything around them. They naturally take time in their day to notice a tree or laugh at a bird or smile at someone in a store. Doing this means we are living in the present moment with an awareness of our surroundings. So put the phone in your pocket and describe your surroundings to yourself as you walk somewhere. If you're in a city, it could be a description of the people you can see, or the traffic around you, the offices or stores you are passing. Begin to connect with others by giving them a smile. If you are in nature, describe the trees to yourself: "There are several trees. They are really tall. The first one has a massive trunk and a thick canopy of leaves. Some of the leaves are brown, and there are leaves on the ground that sound crunchy underfoot."

When you do this, you will notice that the head-chatter disappears as you are focussed on what is in your surroundings and learning to be in the here and now.

A Quick Tip: If you are feeling anxious, describe five things that are in your immediate environment to yourself. It will help you to feel better.

**Meditation and Yoga**

Meditation is also beneficial for relaxation. There are many types of meditation, and should you want to explore this, you can find a class locally or investigate the many different online possibilities, including apps and YouTube videos. When first beginning to meditate, you may find guided meditations the easiest to follow. If you search "meditation with Carolyn in Hawaii," on YouTube, you will find some meditations I recorded that you may enjoy.

Yoga is another great way of learning to be present in the moment and relax the physical body as well as the mind. Yoga can be done at a class or at home from online sources.

Have an open mind and be playful, experimenting with things that help you to relax.

## ∾ NOTES ∾

_____

_____

_____

_____

_____

_____

_____

_____

_____

_____

_____

_____

_____

_____

_____

_____

# CHAPTER NINE

## Sleep and the Notebook Technique

Many people with anxiety experience poor or disturbed sleep patterns causing them to wake up each day feeling tired. This further perpetuates the cycle of anxiety because when we are tired, our coping mechanisms are weakened.

Some people find that they fall asleep quickly at night, but if they wake up during the night to use the bathroom, they cannot get back to sleep because of racing thoughts. Others find they wake up multiple times during the night with persistent thoughts preventing them from getting back to sleep. Some people find they have difficulty getting off to sleep when they go to bed because their mind just won't shut off.

If you think about the unconscious mind being like a five-year-old, you can imagine the five-year-old tugging on your leg trying to get your attention. During the day you may be busy and not resolve the thoughts that are running around in your mind, but at night when you finally fall asleep, the five-year-old is left juggling all of those thoughts and wakes you up to check: "What are you going to do about this? Have you remembered to do that? Did you call xxx? Did you buy fruit today?"

Perhaps you've seen a plate spinning act at a circus or on TV. The performer runs around the stage with plates spinning on posts, working to keep all of the plates in motion so that they don't drop to the ground and break. Your unconscious mind is doing something similar at night. It's keeping all the thoughts running until it thinks you have dealt with them.

There is a simple solution to this problem:

**The Notebook Technique**

Keep a notebook by your bedside. Before you go to sleep at night, write down a maximum of ten bullet points (thoughts that are running through your mind). We are not writing long sentences, just brief bullet points. It could be as simple as "I need eggs" or "Joan was grumpy today" or "highway was busy" or "kids need toothbrushes." Then close the book and do the Sensory Relaxation Process that we learned in the last chapter. It's printed again here for you.

When you wake up during the night, don't turn your light on, simply grab the notebook and your pen, and jot down a maximum of ten bullet points of things that are running through your mind. It does not matter how or where you write these in your notebook because you are not going to re-read them. All that matters is that you write them down.

Then close the book and do the Sensory Relaxation Process.

Sit or lie down in your bed.

Pick a spot out in front of you which is up above eye level (e.g. where the wall meets the ceiling or a spot on the ceiling). Roll your eyes up and focus on that spot, allowing your vision to expand around to the sides (peripheral vision).

Whilst still looking at the spot:

Concentrate on noticing four different things you can see in your peripheral vision, such as colors, shapes, or objects.

Then listen closely for four sounds that you can hear around you.

Still staring at that spot, focus on four things you can feel, such as your breathing, chair, clothing, hands, or feet.

Close your eyes.

Remember three things you saw around you.

Listen carefully for three sounds around you.

Focus on three things that you can feel.

Open your eyes and focus on the same spot, expanding your peripheral vision again.

Notice two things you can see in your peripheral vision.

Listen for two sounds around you.

And still staring at that spot, focus on two things you can feel.

Close your eyes.

Remember one thing you saw,

Listen carefully for one new sound or the sound of your breathing.

Focus on the sensation of your breathing.

At night, in the dark, it may not be possible to see four things; if that is the case, please imagine four things that could be there. The exercise will work just the same. Similarly, if there are not four sounds that you can hear, imagine four things that you might hear, such as the wind outside or the sound of a dog or cat.

You may find it helpful to record yourself speaking the relaxation exercise into the voice memo section on your phone so that you can just listen to it.

If you practice this technique every night, you should find that within two-to-three weeks you will be sleeping better, not waking up as much during the night, and able to go back to sleep much quicker if you do get up to go to the bathroom.

With this technique you are allowing the mind to let go and relax, knowing that anything you have written down, you have dealt with so it doesn't have to keep reminding you.

One important thing to be aware of is whether we are doing "what-if" thoughts about having a bad night. Once we have experienced several nights of poor sleep, we may get into a thinking pattern during the afternoon or evening: "What if I have a bad night tonight? What if I don't sleep well tonight? What if I'm tired again tomorrow?" Now as we have learned in Chapter Four, not only does your unconscious mind think that this is already happening and release the stress chemicals into your body, but focusing on the negative also attracts it to you and makes it more likely to be true. Instead of the negative "what-if" thoughts, make sure that you are focusing on positive "what-if" thoughts: "What if I sleep well tonight? What if I have a great night? What if I have lots of energy tomorrow and feel great?"

Now remember that consciously you may not believe this, but your unconscious mind needs to hear it.

In addition to the Notebook Technique and ensuring the negative "what-ifs" are turned around, all of the usual things that can help us to have a good night sleep are still relevant:

- Switching off your blue screen devices and not having them in bed.
- Switching off the TV and preferably not having a TV in the bedroom
- Drinking something warm and comforting like a herbal tea that is caffeine free
- Taking a warm shower prior to getting into bed
- Reading a book in bed for pleasure
- Taking a walk around the block in the early evening
- Listening to some relaxing music
- Ensuring your room is dark
- Ensuring your room is a cool and comfortable temperature
- Using a white noise device if you are in a noisy environment

If you have difficulty sleeping at night or staying asleep, begin using the Notebook Technique and the Sensory Relaxation Process from this chapter, and I'm sure you will begin to sleep better within a short period.

# ∞ NOTES ∞

# CHAPTER TEN

## Dealing with Grief

Grief is a natural response to loss: the loss of a partner, a pet, or another loved one; the end of a relationship; the loss of a job; moving to a different town and leaving the familiar life behind; the loss of physical mobility following an accident or injury. Any type of loss causes the emotional response of grief. Sudden unexpected death with no opportunity to say goodbye exacerbates grief and often leads to anxiety. The more significant the loss, the more intense the grief will be. Whatever the loss is, we need to give ourselves time to process our feelings and find a new way living without what we've lost.

If we have experienced multiple types/episodes of loss, there may be residual grief and stress that has not been resolved. This combined with some of the other factors we have already explored in this book can lead to intense anxiety.

When we feel as though we have no control in a particular environment or situation--for example, the loss of a spouse, getting let go from a job, experiencing a serious illness, surviving an accident or a heart attack-- we may feel anxious about what is going to happen in the future. "Will I be able to get another job? What if someone else dies? What if I die? What if I can't trust my body any more?"

In many cases grief may be stacked from several events, for example, having lost a grandparent when you were a child and not having been allowed at the funeral, having lost a friend to an accident with no opportunity to say goodbye, and then perhaps losing a parent or other loved one. If the grief from each event has not been dealt with, then we are likely to trigger the grief from the earlier events along with the latest one, and it may appear that the grief for this latest loss is insurmountable. When this happens, negative thought patterns may occur such as "I lose everyone I love" or "What if something happens to my kids/partner/friend?"

If we think back to the story of Jeremiah in the first chapter, he told me: "Just last year I lost a good friend and my father. I don't think I've had a chance to grieve properly because I've been so busy !"

So one of the first things to do if you have lost someone, even if it was twenty years ago, is to write a Grief Letter.

## Grief Letter

It is important to write the letter by hand on paper rather than on a computer or phone. In the Grief Letter, write down everything and anything that you would want to say to that person, good, bad, indifferent. No one is going to read this letter, and it's important that you express everything you want or need to say.

Write this letter over a period of three days, each day re-read it, add to it or delete parts; then on day three when you are finished, either burn the letter, bury it, or rip it into shreds and dispose of it. It is very important that you actually dispose of it on day three and do not leave it in a journal or notepad.

The unconscious mind loves rituals and the ritual of burning/burying/ripping up the letter symbolises that you are letting go of something. When you write this Grief Letter, you may be surprised what comes up for you, including things you thought you had dealt with. Allow yourself a little time each day to grieve, and then on day three, be ready to let go.

Do this process for each person that you have lost. I also recommend writing a Grief Letter if a relationship has ended, if you have lost a job that you loved, if you have left behind a place/friends you loved, or if you have lost your lifestyle due to a physical injury or illness.

The ability to let go of the things that you were holding onto will decrease your stress levels and reduce your anxiety. If the loss of a loved one is recent, you may find comfort in writing another Grief Letter to the same person after a month or so.

It's important to be aware of any negative "what-if's"and any other negative thoughts you may be entertaining as these lead into anxiety; if you notice them, work through them as outlined in the previous chapters.

## New Routines

Sometimes people find that they're clinging on to an old routine that they used to have when the loved one was still alive or prior to the move, accident, or injury. We cling onto the routine as a way of trying to stay in our comfort zone. If something happens to disrupt that routine or it becomes no longer viable, we may become anxious as we can't control our environment and worry about what might happen or what could go wrong.

For this reason, it's important to begin to create new routines for yourself. Cultivate new interests and new friendships regardless of the type of loss, and start to focus on what you want, what you can do, and what you have in your life that is positive. Creating new routines enables us to grow and move forward. Any situation of loss is an opportunity to grow and create new things in our lives. You are not minimizing the memory of the person for whom you are grieving by creating new things in your life or meeting new people.

During the first session with Jeremiah when we discovered what the probable causes of his anxiety were, I explained how to do the Grief Letter and asked him to write one for his friend in the first week. I also taught him how to do the Sensory Relaxation Process and advised him to practice it every day once he got home from work. We discussed his breathing, and he learned the 5x5 Breathing Process to use during the day and in situations where he felt anxious.

When Jeremiah came back for the second session, he reported that he didn't realise how much he had been hanging onto in relation to the death of his friend; the letter really helped him to finally feel as though he had grieved. Jeremiah said he had felt a little self-conscious doing 5x5 Breathing during the day at work; however, he persevered and realized that nobody was actually watching him anyway.

At the second session I asked Jeremiah to write a Grief Letter for his father. We also discussed his perfectionism and high expectations of colleagues. Jeremiah agreed to drop his expectations by 10% in the coming week. We also introduced the Notebook Technique to enable Jeremiah to sleep better at night now that he was comfortable doing the Sensory Relaxation Process. Throughout each session, we also discussed and explored "what-if" thinking and other negative thoughts.

By session three, Jeremiah reported that he had already started to feel a lot better. He was recognising the situations at work where he was being a perfectionist, and although it was difficult, he had managed to let go of checking up on his colleagues' work or redoing reports before submitting them. He had also become aware of the never-ending stream of "what-if" thoughts that he was entertaining. Although his mind still raced at times, he was getting better at turning the thoughts around and noticed that they were diminishing.

# ༄ NOTES ༄

# CHAPTER ELEVEN

## Magical Tips and Tricks

Neuro Linguistic Programming (NLP) looks at how things are programmed in the mind and how they can be changed to achieve excellence. It often feels like magic. There are some "magical" techniques I'd like to share with you that can reduce the feeling of anxiety very quickly. My clients are often surprised at just how effective these magical techniques are.

**Exercise 1: Change it Out**

If you are feeling anxious, go through this exercise quickly without thinking too much about the answers; go with the first thing that pops into your mind.

Let's look at an example:

First get in touch with that anxious feeling:

Who or what does that feeling remind you of?

_____ "concrete block"

If that feeling had a color, what color would it be?

_____ "red"

If that feeling had a shape, what shape would it be?

_____ "square"

If that feeling had a texture, what texture would it be?

_____ "rough/spiky"

If that feeling had a sound, what sound would it be?

_____ "chalk scratching on a board" "

Is that feeling heavy or light?

_____ "heavy"

Now turn the elements you described into the opposite:

Imagine the concrete block disintegrating and turning into a soft cloud.

Turn the square into a round or puffy shape.

Now have the color red fade into white until there is only white or pale pink.

Erase the rough/spiky texture until it becomes smooth.

Turn down the volume of the chalk scratching and bring in the soothing sounds of ocean waves.

Turn the heavy into light.

Now snap your fingers or imagine the sound of a Tupperware lid snapping on a container to lock the new representation in place.

Practicing this technique can enable you to feel much better in less than five minutes. Of course, the underlying issues have not yet been been dealt with and still need to be addressed, but you can reduce or eliminate the feeling, enabling you to get through your day easier.

Here is a blank form so that you can practice this exercise:

First get in touch with that anxious feeling:

Who or what does that feeling remind you of?

( write your answer here) _____

If that feeling had a color, what color would it be?

_____

If that feeling had a shape, what shape would it be?

_____

If that feeling had a texture, what texture would it be?

_____

If that feeling had a sound, what sound would it be?

_____

Is it heavy or light?

_____

Now go ahead and talk yourself through changing the elements as we did in the example above. Change the elements into things that are pleasing to you.

Imagine the _____ turning into_____

Now have the color fade or merge into_____

until there is only _____ (new color)

Turn the (old shape)_____into a _____
(new shape)

Change the _____ (old texture) until it

becomes _____ (new texture)

Turn down the volume of the (old sound) _____

and bring in the soothing sounds of _____
(new sound)

Turn the heavy into light (or light into lighter)

Once you have your new representation that feels better, make an audible sound to lock it into place.

**Exercise 2: Over the Horizon**

Let's look at an example:

Close your eyes and notice that anxiety. As you notice that anxiety, do you have a picture?

Is that picture black-and-white or color?

_____ "color"

Can you see yourself in the picture or are you looking out through your own eyes?

_____ "looking out through my own eyes"

Is it bright or dim? _____ "bright"

What size is the picture? _____"life-size"

Is it focused or defocused? _____ "focused"

Is it near or far?_____ "near"

Good, now I want you to fade the color out; turn it into black-and-white like an old photograph.

See yourself in the picture, like looking at a photo.

Dim the image like someone has turned the lights out.

Begin shrinking the image down to the size of a postage stamp, and as you do, allow it to become defocused.

Now send that small dark image out over the horizon becoming smaller and smaller until it disappears.

How do you feel now?

## How does this work?

The objective here is to disempower the image. If your image is black-and-white, notice whether it becomes stronger or weaker if you turn it into color; then choose the option that seems weaker.

The same applies for brightness; if your image is already dim, notice what happens if you make it bright. Does this make it feel weaker or stronger? Choose the option that feels weakest.

If your image was already defocussed, check how it feels if you make it focussed; always choose the option that diminishes the anxiety.

Always make sure you can see yourself in the picture like a photograph, always shrink the image to a postage stamp or smaller, and always send it out over the horizon

Here is your worksheet for the exercise:

Close your eyes and notice that anxiety. Do you have a picture?

Is that picture black-and-white or color? _____

Can you see yourself in the picture or are you looking out through your own eyes? _____

Is it bright or dim? _____

What size is the picture?_____

Is it focused or defocused? _____

Is it near or far?_____

Good, now I want you to fade the color out; turn it into black-and-white like an old photograph. Or if it's black-and-white turn it into color; keep whichever representation is the least empowered.

See yourself in the picture, like looking at a photo.

Dim the image like someone has turned the lights out, or if it's dim make it bright. Choose whichever representation is least empowered.

Allow the image to become defocused (fuzzy). If it's already defocused, check what happens if you make it focused. Keep the least empowered representation.

Begin shrinking the image down to the size of a postage stamp and now send that small image out over the horizon becoming smaller and smaller until it disappears

How do you feel now? _____

## Exercise 3: Resource Anchor

This technique enables us to build a resource of powerful positive states such as happiness, laughter, calm, joy, confidence, or relaxation, and then use this resource to override the anxious feeling.

Many professional sports people use this technique to get or keep themselves in "the zone" so they can excel at their sport regardless of what is going on. It keeps them focused.

Anytime we create a specific unique gesture and then link that touch to a state (happiness, laughter, calm, joy, confidence, or relaxation), we are creating an "anchor"-- a neurological link that can be replicated.

For example, putting your index finger and thumb together, or pressing your index finger gently on the index finger knuckle of your other hand, are both specific unique gestures that we can replicate at any time. Choose one of these two options for your Resource Anchor.

To build a resource of goodies for yourself, whenever you find yourself naturally feeling good-- maybe laughing at a movie, your kids, or something funny--make the specific unique gesture (always the same one). Do this for approximately ten seconds (only while you are laughing) and then release. Each time you find yourself laughing at something do the same thing for ten seconds.

If you feel happy or joyful about something, press your anchor for ten seconds while you are in the happy or joyful feeling.

If you feel calm or safe, press your anchor for ten seconds while you are in the calm or safe feeling.

If you are relaxed--such as during a massage or when watching TV, reading a book, or relaxing in bed--press your anchor for ten seconds while you are enjoying the relaxed feeling.

If you are feeling confident--perhaps you got good feedback at work or know you look great or did something well--press your anchor for ten seconds while you are in that confident feeling.

Aim to build at least ten positive states onto your anchor. These can be a combination of different states as listed above or ten of one state such as laughter. Just use whatever you are experiencing that is positive to build the resource anchor. Be sure to use the same touch in the same place each time.

Make a list below as you build your anchor so you know when you've got to ten.

1. _____

2. _____

3. _____

4. _____

5. _____

6. _____

7. _____

8. _____

9. _____

10. _____

Once you have at least ten positives on your anchor, then you can use it if you begin to feel anxiety coming on. As soon as you notice the negative feeling, press your anchor for approximately twenty seconds (same anchor, same touch) and notice what happens. You will notice that the anxious feeling diminishes or is replaced by a more positive feeling. If you don't notice anything, it means you don't yet have enough powerful resource states built into the anchor or you have not been using the same touch (specific unique gesture) in the same place to build your anchor.

The Resource Anchor was used by Brad whom we met in Chapter Eight to help him overcome his anxiety around flying.

Have fun with this magical technique, it really works! I created a giggle anchor during my first NLP training in 2001, and it still works; I can giggle anytime I choose simply by pressing my anchor!

## Other Tips:

### Avoid Television

I recommend that all my clients avoid watching the news and any horror/murder-mystery type shows for at least two weeks when they first start working on eliminating anxiety. The unconscious mind can't tell the difference between whether you are watching something or it's happening to you, and as your stress levels are already high, it's important not to raise them any higher. Watch funny shows, things that make you laugh or feel good.

### Caffeine

Please avoid caffeine laden energy drinks and things with guarana as they exacerbate anxiety and increase palpitations. Your morning coffee is fine, but keep it to one cup or switch to decaf for a few weeks.

### Physical Exercise

If you are feeling uncomfortable, perhaps a feeling of unease in the stomach or a feeling of adrenaline surging through your body, physical exercise can help. As you recall, the feelings you are experiencing are due to the fight-and-flight chemicals being present in your body, often in copious amounts. If there were truly something dangerous occurring, you would use those chemicals to fight or run. This is where physical exercise can be beneficial. Go for a brisk jog or walk around the block. If you cannot go outside, simply do ten or fifteen jumping jacks in your lounge room or kitchen; if you have a punching bag, spend five-to-ten minutes using it. You can choose any form of physical exercise that you want and do it briskly for ten-to-fifteen minutes while making sure you are telling yourself positive thoughts.

# ∾ NOTES ∾

# CHAPTER TWELVE

## Case Studies

Having read the book up until this point, you can see that anxiety is not a one-size-fits-all matter. Everyone is unique, and by creating your own individual recipe for success, you can address the variety of things that have led to your anxiety. Once you start to take action in a positive way, the results begin to snowball, and suddenly you realise that you had a good morning or a better day, or that last night you slept better, or that the uncomfortable feeling in your stomach has subsided. By continuing to apply the exercises that are relevant to your situation, you can be assured that change happens!

Because you are now armed with the new knowledge gained from reading this book, you will find that you become more aware of what is occurring when you are in situations where you feel uncomfortable. You will easily notice yourself slipping into an old pattern, such as not saying NO. With awareness comes the ability to create new outcomes by implementing the strategies learned.

Let's reconnect with some of the clients we met earlier in the book. They are just a handful of the hundreds of clients I've worked with over the years who have successfully implemented the strategies I've shared with you. In Chapter One, you met Megan and Jeremiah, both of whom were struggling with anxiety. Let's find out how their journeys progressed:

**Megan**

Megan was a married working mom with two children. She was finding it hard to deal with the kids and the house on top of working a job. Megan constantly felt as though she had a knot in her stomach; she dreaded going to work and wasn't sleeping properly. She had thoughts running through her head all the time and felt exhausted.

In my first session with Megan, we went through the questions from Chapter Three to determine which areas she needed to focus on in order to overcome her anxiety. Here are the questions again:

- Are you a perfectionist?
- Do you have high expectations of yourself and-or others?

- Are you the strong one? The person other people come to for advice and help or to offload their problems on?
- Do you have difficulty saying no?
- Have one or both of your parents suffered from anxiety?
- Has there been an incident or incidents in the last two to three years where you have been out of control either due to an illness or injury, or due to something that's happened in your environment, to you, or people close to you?
- Have any loved ones passed away recently?

Then we chose the exercises that relate to those areas and added them to her recipe for success:

1. What-if Thoughts from Chapter Four (Everyone does this.)
2. 5x5 Breathing from Chapter Seven (Everyone does this.)
3. Sensory Relaxation from Chapter Eight (Everyone does this.)
4. Treat Yourself Kindly from Chapter Four
5. Notebook Technique from Chapter Nine (for poor sleep)
6. Change it Out Technique from Chapter Eleven (for knot in stomach)
7. Over the Horizon Technique from Chapter Eleven (for knot in stomach)

Megan was using a lot of what-if thoughts: "What if I have a bad day at work? What if one of my kids gets sick and I have to leave work to pick them up? What if my boss asks me to work late? What if my boss isn't happy with my work? What if my husband is fed up of me always being tired?" She was also telling herself, "I'm a bad mom. I'm a bad wife. I'm a bad employee. I always look a mess."

So the first thing we started working on was the "what-if thoughts" and turning the "I'm not ..." thoughts into positive affirmations. We also added the Sensory Relaxation Process and 5x5 Breathing in week one.

Megan had difficulty making time for herself every day to put into practice the elements needed to eliminate her anxiety. Like most people, she had great intentions; however, she would easily get distracted by the needs of her children, her boss at work, and the busy-ness of her life! Sometimes she would think, "It's not so bad. It will go away. We all have our problem; this is just mine." Part of her believed that it would be selfish to put herself first and take time to do the exercises. She also worried, "What if it doesn't work? It might work for others and not me. Maybe nothing will help."

After several weeks of intending to do the exercises and then feeling dismayed that yet another week had gone by without any change, she finally realised that she really did have to start making the changes herself to experience improvement. Once she started working on her thoughts, she was surprised to notice how many negative thoughts she was thinking. She found the easiest way to check in on herself was to think of her unconscious mind as a five-year-old; her son Alex was six, so she would ask herself, "Could I say this to Alex and have him be happy and healthy?" If the answer was no, she would change the thought.

Megan found the breathing helpful throughout her day at work and enjoyed using humming and chanting as a way to feel better at home. At first, her kids thought it was funny that she was humming tunes at home, but then they joined in! She loved using the Change it Out and Over the Horizon Techniques to reduce the knot in her stomach before she went to work or even at work if she needed it.

Four weeks after starting to work with her thoughts and the other strategies, Megan noticed she no longer had the knot in her stomach and didn't need to use the Change it Out or Over the Horizon Techniques anymore. She had also started employing the Notebook Technique at night and was beginning to notice an improvement in her sleep, enabling her to wake up feeling refreshed rather than constantly exhausted. By the end of eight weeks. Megan let me know that she was feeling "normal" again and having fun with her kids and husband again. She regretted the wasted weeks when she had been resisting doing the exercises, but said she was "so happy" that she had finally "got it." She knew she had to remain mindful of her thought processes and be kind to herself but was really enjoying feeling good again.

## Jeremiah

Jeremiah was a successful business man in his mid-forties. He loved to work out but was having trouble with heart palpitations, a racing feeling in his body, and continual thoughts running through his mind. At times he felt like he couldn't breathe and was unable to relax. He had difficulty sleeping. Going through the questions from Chapter Three, we ascertained that Jeremiah was a perfectionist and had high expectations of himself and others. He had lost both his father and his friend in the past year.

This is the plan of action we created for Jeremiah:

1. What-if Thoughts from Chapter Four (Everyone does this.)
2. 5x5 Breathing from Chapter Seven (Everyone does this.)
3. Sensory Relaxation from Chapter Eight (Everyone does this.)
4. Grief Letters to his father and friend from Chapter Ten
5. Reducing Perfectionism from Chapter Five
6. Changing Words of Pressure into Words of Choice from Chapter Four
7. Notebook Technique from Chapter Nine
8. Being Present from Chapter Eight
9. Meditation from Chapter Eight
10. Humming and Chanting from Chapter Seven

During the first session with Jeremiah when we discovered what the probable causes of his anxiety were, I explained how to do the Grief Letter and asked him to write one for his friend in the first week. I also taught him how to do the Sensory Relaxation Process and asked him to practice it every day once he got home from work. We discussed his breathing, and he learned the 5x5 Breathing Process to use during the day and in situations in which he felt anxious. Jeremiah also agreed to cut out the energy drinks he was having after the gym each day (as recommended in Chapter Eleven).

When Jeremiah came back for the second session, he reported that he didn't realise how much he had been hanging onto in relation to the death of his friend; the letter really helped him to finally feel as though he had grieved. Jeremiah said he had felt a little self-conscious doing 5x5 Breathing during the day at work; however, he persevered and realized that nobody was watching him anyway. He noted that the frequency and severity of his palpitations were reducing.

At the second session I asked Jeremiah to write a Grief Letter for his father. We also discussed his perfectionism and high expectations of colleagues. Jeremiah agreed to drop his expectations by 10% in the coming week. We introduced the Notebook Technique to enable Jeremiah to sleep better at night now that he was comfortable doing the Sensory Relaxation Process. Throughout each session we also discussed and explored "what-if" thinking and other negative thoughts.

By session three, Jeremiah reported that he had already started to feel a lot better. He was recognising the situations at work where he was being a perfectionist, and although it was difficult, he had managed to let go of checking up on his colleagues' work or redoing reports before submitting them. He had also become aware of the never-ending stream of "what-if" thoughts that he was entertaining. Although his mind still raced at times, he was getting better at turning the thoughts around and noticed that they were diminishing.

At session three, we introduced changing Words of Pressure to Words of Choice. This was a big one for Jeremiah as he constantly used Words of Pressure when working out. He was surprised to find how much more he enjoyed his daily gym sessions once he changed his language. He also started working on being present. In the evenings, Jeremiah began experimenting with meditations on YouTube and was surprised at how much he enjoyed them; he noticed that meditation really stopped all of his head-chatter and finally enabled him to feel calm.

By the end of six weeks Jeremiah reported that he was "doing great." He was calm and relaxed, sleeping well, and enjoying life again.

Nine months after our first session, Jeremiah sent me a message thanking me for my help and telling me that he loved meditation so much he had trained to be a meditation instructor and was now running a weekly meditation at his gym! He was happy that his anxiety had led him to something that he loved and would never otherwise have contemplated.

## Mary

Mary is the lady we met in Chapter Five. She was in her fifties and had been married ten years to her second husband. Mary presented with anxiety, and when we went through the questions in Chapter Three, we discovered that she was a perfectionist, a person whom other people come to for advice and to "dump" their problems on. Mary's mother had anxiety and took medications for many years to control it. Mary had a long history of not being able to say NO to friends who asked for help, nor to her husband, so she frequently found herself doing things she really didn't want to do or going places she had no interest in.

Mary's recipe for success:

1. What-if Thoughts from Chapter Four (Everyone does this.)
2. 5x5 Breathing from Chapter Seven (Everyone does this.)
3. Sensory Relaxation from Chapter Eight (Everyone does this.)
4. Reducing Perfectionism from Chapter Five
5. Being Kind to Yourself from Chapter Four
6. Boundaries and Saying NO from Chapter Six
7. Being Present from Chapter Eight
8. Tips from Chapter Eleven (TV)

During the first week Mary started working with the Sensory Relaxation Process to reduce her stress levels, the 5x5 Breathing Process, the what-if thoughts, and reducing perfectionism by 10%. As soon as she discovered how upset her husband was by her behavior of re-doing everything he had done, she stopped the behavior immediately; she was quite shocked as she had no idea he had been affected by her actions. Mary found it quite a challenge to reduce her perfectionism in other areas, but she continued to be mindful of it and work on it.

In the second week, we added in the exercises on Setting Boundaries and Saying NO. Mary was hesitant to say NO to things her husband suggested as they were going through a rough patch in their marriage, and she feared it would make things worse. In fact, once she began saying NO, her husband was relieved, as it enabled him to do certain activities by himself or with friends rather than Mary being resentful feeling she "had to" go. Now when she says yes to something, he knows she is genuinely happy to be doing the activity with him. Mary found it easier to say NO to requests from friends and was happy to find it didn't negatively affect her friendships. Mary also stopped watching the news and murder-mystery shows; she was a big fan of murder-mystery shows and had not previously been aware of the impact they were having on her anxiety

In week three, Mary added in Being Kind to Yourself. She was surprised to discover the impact her words were having on her well being. Her mother had always had high expectations of her and had been quite critical of anything Mary did; in fact, her mother had never told Mary she was proud of her. Being kind to herself remains something Mary consciously needs to be mindful of. Mary loved the Being Present Exercise and found it to be very helpful in bringing her into the now. She goes into her garden much more now as she finds it a place where it's easy to be present and relax.

By the end of the fourth week, Mary was feeling significantly better. She was still a work in progress, but she knew she was on the right track and moving forward.

## John

John was one of my clients in Australia. He was great at working with cars and enjoyed tinkering with his old MG at home for fun. Over the years, friends and acquaintances started to ask him to check their cars or fix them. John, brought up to always be helpful to others, would automatically say yes even if it meant he lost out on time with his wife and kids at the weekend or if it meant that he didn't have time to work on his own car. Eventually he became so fed up that he didn't want to work on cars at all, and he became anxious when friends called in case it was another job he didn't have time to do. He found himself not wanting to socialize as he felt obligated to say yes to his friends if they asked for help.

After going through the questions in Chapter Three, we began working with the exercises for establishing boundaries and saying NO.

John's recipe for success:

1. What-if thoughts from Chapter Four (Everyone does this.)
2. 5x5 Breathing from Chapter Seven (Everyone does this.)
3. Sensory Relaxation from Chapter Eight (Everyone does this.)
4. Boundaries and Saying NO from Chapter Six
5. Over the Horizon Technique from Chapter Eleven

John worried that his friends wouldn't like him or respect him if he said NO to helping them; however, he found that his true friends respected him for being honest.

He started using the Sensory Relaxation Process, 5x5 Breathing, and also the Over the Horizon Technique. He found all of them useful for reducing his anxious feelings. Over the next few weeks, he was also mindful of any "what-if" thoughts and worked to turn them around.

Several months later he reported back to me that his life was back on track. He had time to go out and have fun with the kids and his wife; they were even planning a vacation. Yes, he had lost two "friends," but he realised they weren't true friends anyway. They were only there when they needed something from him. John told me that he had also started saying NO to extra work loads at his job and was much happier.

**Gemma**

We met Gemma in Chapter Six. Gemma was in her late twenties. She worked for a large company and really wanted to get a promotion. In order to achieve this, she said yes to everything that was asked of her. She spent evenings and weekends at work and was beginning to feel overwhelmed, resentful, and anxious. She rarely had time to go out with her friends and said she felt "like a hamster on a wheel," always running but never getting anywhere.

We created her recipe for success at the first session:

1. What-if Thoughts from Chapter Four (Everyone does this.)
2. 5x5 Breathing from Chapter Seven (Everyone does this.)
3. Sensory Relaxation from Chapter Eight (Everyone does this.)
4. Saying NO and Setting Boundaries from Chapter Six
5. Changing Words of Pressure into Words of Choice from Chapter Four
6. Notebook Technique from Chapter Nine
7. Humming from Chapter Seven
8. Resource Anchor from Chapter Eleven
9. Tip about caffeine from Chapter Eleven

When we first talked about boundaries, Gemma was very reluctant to change her ways. She really did believe that saying yes to everything her boss asked her to do would put her line for the promotion.

However, Gemma worked on her negative "what-if's," and found that humming soothed her and made her feel calmer. We discovered that Gemma often drank two coffees in the morning and at least two energy drinks in the afternoon; once we discussed the impact of these on her anxiety, she stopped the energy drinks and cut her coffee down to one a day. Gemma began using the Notebook Technique at night and found that her sleep was improving.

She was beginning to feel better, but she still spent all her time at work. The crunch came at the end of the third week when someone else who had been at the company for only six months was given the promotion. To add insult to injury, Gemma was asked if she could help the new employee settle into the new role!

Gemma ended up taking two weeks off work for stress leave. During this time, she started working on the ways to put her boundaries in place. She also decided to start looking for other jobs. Gemma started working on changing her use of "should, must, and have to" into Words of Choice. At this stage, we built a Resource Anchor of confidence, personal power, happiness, and calm that she could use when she went back to work or to interviews.

Once Gemma went back to work, she used her Resource Anchor to feel confident enough to say NO to some of the tasks that were asked of her. She also used the "Do I want to? Do I personally need to? And for what purpose would I do it?" questions and thus decided to go home at six pm every evening regardless of whether she had finished her tasks for the day or not. She also stopped working weekends.

Gemma was surprised and delighted at how much better she felt. Her anxiety was diminishing, her social life was improving, and although she had been looking at other jobs, she was offered a promotion at her own company within four months of having changed her way of doing things. Gemma reported back to me, "If I had known that saying NO and enforcing my boundaries would work so well, I would have implemented it the first time we talked about it."

**Brad**

Our last client is Brad whom we met in Chapter Seven. Brad was anxious about flying. He had to fly frequently for work, and he had reached the point where he was contemplating changing jobs because he no longer wanted to travel. He loved his job, yet had started feeling anxious every time he was on a plane.

Asking the questions from Chapter Three had highlighted that Brad had become a father nine months previously and since then had been anxious about flying in case anything happened to him, leaving his wife and child alone. He had never had a bad experience flying but had a friend in high school years ago who had lost his father in a light aircraft crash. (Brad did not personally know his friend's father so there was no need for a Grief Letter.)

Brad's recipe for success:

1.  What-if Thoughts from Chapter Four (Everyone does this.)
2.  5x5 Breathing from Chapter Seven (Everyone does this.)
3.  Sensory Relaxation from Chapter Eight
4.  Being Present from Chapter Eight
5.  Resource Anchor from Chapter Eleven

The combination of turning the negative "what if" thoughts around, using the Sensory Relaxation Process and 5x5 Breathing cleared the anxiety; he found himself able to travel comfortably again.

At first, when he was looking at his what-if thought of "What if I'm in a plane crash and my wife has to cope without me?" he asked himself, "Do I have proof?"and answered, "Yes, because Tom's dad died." I explained that that is not proof that it will happen to him right now in the present moment; it's simply something from the past which holds no proof for today. Once he understood this, he found it easier to get rid of the "what-ifs."

Brad created a Resource Anchor with "happy, laughter, confident, relaxed" (ten separate events) and used this the first two times he went on a plane. He found that he didn't need to use it after that.

After just four weeks Brad was flying comfortably again. He was extremely happy as it meant he could keep his job. He had also become aware of negative "what-ifs" he had been doing in other areas of his life and was successfully stopping himself from worrying about things that haven't happened yet and may never happen.

In reading these stories about real clients that I have had the pleasure of working with, I hope you may find some similarities with your own situation and also understand exactly how to create and use your own personal recipe for success.

# ❦ NOTES ❦

# CHAPTER THIRTEEN

## Keeping the Peace

In the last chapter we completed the stories of my clients whom you met throughout the book: real clients who eliminated their anxiety and were able to get on with their lives again.

In case any of you are wondering about the story of my first husband from Chapter One, he successfully survived his bone marrow transplant, which sadly was not the case for the other patient in the transplant unit at that time. After a year of recovering and carefully rebuilding his immune system, he was able to get on with life again. It has now been 34 years since the transplant, and he is still happy and healthy.

Once you've eliminated your anxiety, it's important to continue to regularly do things for yourself to keep your stress levels down and to promote physical, mental, emotional, and spiritual wellbeing.

Over the years I've discovered that I love chanting. You can do it almost anywhere: in the house, in the car, at the beach (if there's not too many people), anywhere out in nature. I began listening to the relaxing music of Sacred Earth, an Australian husband-and-wife team (Jethro and Prem) who sing devotional music. I started to explore chanting with "Om mane padme om" and also just "Om". Eventually, I attended kirtan evenings in Australia where they were chanting Krishna chants. I began learning Hawaiian chants when I was first introduced to the Hawaiian culture in 2005. No matter what you chant, it resonates deep within the soul, switches the body into its parasympathetic or healing mode, and simply feels good!

I also enjoy meditation and often start my day with a short guided meditation. (Deepak Chopra is one of my favorites as I find his voice soothing.)

Now that you've read this book, discovered your own specific recipe for success to eliminate anxiety, and started putting the exercises, tips, and techniques into practice, you are truly on the road to reclaiming your life and getting back to being your best self. What changes have you already noticed?

Write them here:

1. _____

2. _____

3. _____

4. _____

5. _____

Stop for a moment and take a deep breath; recognize just how far you have already come and how good your life is going to be in the future! Be proud and acknowledge yourself for having started the journey back to wellbeing.

Yes, eliminating anxiety takes some work, but it is undoubtedly worth it to be able to move on with your life and step into a whole new way of being. By implementing the tips, techniques, and exercises, you will gain an awareness of the behaviors, events, or situations that may be triggers for you. That awareness will enable you to be proactive in dealing with things without becoming anxious in the future. Keeping this book as a tool even after you've eliminated your anxiety will enable you to access the resources any time you need to in the future.

Sometimes there are unexpected benefits that arise from using the strategies in this book, as happened with Jeremiah, who became a meditation instructor after using meditation as part of his recipe for success.

By taking a positive and proactive approach to eliminating anxiety, you too can open up the opportunity to bring changes for the better, improving your confidence, resilience, and self-efficacy. It may take a few weeks, but by making the decision to live in the moment, setting aside a little time each day for your own personal wellbeing, you can truly make the changes for yourself which will enable you to experience peace, joy, calm, and happiness once again.

In closing, I want to remind you that I have posted some free resources for you to continue your journey to wellbeing on my website at www.anxietythebook.com and also on the Facebook page: Anxiety the Book (@anxietythebook) where I would love for you to join our community. I love to hear about your success stories and how this book has impacted your life.

I wish you happiness, joy, peace and wellbeing.

With much Aloha, Carolyn

# ∾ NOTES ∾

# You Are Invited!

Carolyn G.A Ching offers retreats, personal sessions and personal breakthrough sessions as well as training courses for Hypnotherapy and NLP practitioners in her hometown of Kailua Kona on the Big Island of Hawaii and throughout the world. You can attend these events.

## Contact me at

carolyn@bigislandhypnosis.com
carolyn@australianhypnosis.com
www.anxietythebook.com

**for information, dates, and locations
--and to change your life today!**

Printed in Great Britain
by Amazon